AVAILABLE WISDOM

Insights from
Beyond the
Third Dimension

....

As told through **JOHN McKIBBIN**
to **GATES McKIBBIN**

LIFELINES LIBRARY

For information, contact:

Field Flowers, Inc.
641 Healdsburg Avenue
Healdsburg, CA 95448
707 433 9771
www.fieldflowers.com

.Cover and text design by Kajun Design

Front cover detail from "Judith II (Salome)"
by Gustav Klimt (Cameraphoto/Art Resource)

Author's photo by Christina Schmidhofer

ISBN 1-929799-05-5

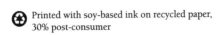 Printed with soy-based ink on recycled paper,
30% post-consumer

To my spiritual teacher, Sri Sathya Sai Baba, who is a perpetual source of profound wisdom and a catalyst for my ongoing enlightenment

Also by Gates McKibbin:

The Light in the Living Room: Dad's Messages from the Other Side

LoveLines: Notes on Loving and Being Loved

A Course in Courage: Disarming the Darkness with Strength of Heart

A Handbook on Hope: Fusing Optimism and Action

The Life of the Soul: The Path of Spirit in Your Lifetimes

What began three years ago as a series of journal entries is now coming into the world as a series of books. All along the way people with the perspective and expertise I needed crossed my path at exactly the right time. Each person has contributed soul and substance to the project. I am abundantly grateful to:

♦ **Ned Engle,** who saw what my writings could become long before I did and then adroitly guided me there.

♦ **Barbra Dillenger, Michael Makay, Benjo Masilungan** and **Anthony Corso,** whose comments on each new manuscript reassured me of the accuracy and usefulness of the material.

♦ **Judith Appelbaum** and **Florence Janovic** at Sensible Solutions, whose savvy counsel about the publishing industry kept me confident and on course.

♦ **Carol Fall,** who offered discerning marketing advice and was the creative force behind the book titles.

♦ **Erin Blackwell** and **Cynthia Rubin,** whose editorial finesse honored and strengthened the messages.

♦ **Laurie Smith** and **Pat Koren** at Kajun Design, who transformed each book into a jewel within and without.

CONTENTS

GLOSSARY

Creation consists of multiple dimensions of reality. Each dimension is characterized by its vibratory or magnetic quality. The higher the frequency at which the dimension vibrates, the more at one it is with God. The **higher realms** are the dimensions of spiritual reality beyond the material world, where distinctions based on time and space do not exist.

Karma is composed of imprints on your soul created by your choices (thoughts, words and actions). Choices that embrace spirit heal, balance, complete and remove karmic imprints from your current and prior lifetimes that distance your soul from God. Choices that deny or avoid spirit add new imprints that must be healed, balanced, completed and removed later.

Your **lesson** is the larger karmic pattern or theme you are addressing during this lifetime.

Your **mission** is the major contribution you are making in this lifetime to enable the evolution of collective consciousness toward oneness with God.

Your **soul** is the vessel for your spirit. It carries an

infinite variety of karmic imprints that record the experiences your spirit has had, in and out of embodiment. Your soul is all love and light. It represents your limitless potential to embrace spirit to the fullest capacity.

Spirit guides are spiritual entities who have committed to helping you follow the path of love and contribute to the spiritual evolution of all creation. They whisper in your ear telepathically. They send you insights and intuitive flashes. They reaffirm your deepest inner knowing that there is a benevolent higher power inherent in all things.

The **third dimension** is the material reality on planet earth. It consists of dense physical matter that vibrates slowly. The third dimension is characterized by segmented linear time (past, present and future) and compartmentalized space (measurements, boundaries and separation).

The **veil** is a magnetic field surrounding planet earth that separates the vibratory capacity of the third dimension from that of the higher realms. It forms a barrier between your earthly awareness and your higher consciousness. The veil creates the illusion that material reality—and your survival in it—is your reason for being.

The term **we** that is used throughout this book refers to John McKibbin, the spirit who was Gates' father in this lifetime, and the other spiritual entities collaborating with him on the messages he sent down to her.

FLYING to the HIGHER REALMS

What are the higher dimensions? How do you access them? What happens to your physical body when your consciousness goes there? How do you know if you have actually tapped into them?

Those are all relevant questions—ones this book answers with descriptions rather than prescriptions. This is not a how-to book for flying off to the upper dimensions. If it offered you a step-by-step list of what to do, it would be suggesting something that is infeasible.

Accessing the higher realms is not a prescribed process that you can follow with your intellect. It is a passage that you undergo with your higher consciousness, often without your observable awareness that it is occurring.

The most important step you can take if you want to reach the higher realms is to live love in the third dimension. This one building block is critical. More than anything else, doing so will enable you to transcend the limitations of the material world. The gateway to the higher dimensions opens to you after you have put love and light at the center of your life—after you have begun to integrate them into your thoughts, words and deeds.

How will you know that you have accessed the dimensions beyond time and space and, more specifically, which one you have entered? There is a simple answer to that: You probably will not know, especially at first. Much of this exploration occurs at night while you are sleeping. That is when your higher consciousness can take flight without the encumbrances of your dominant rational mind. You travel far and wide in the sleep state, collaborating with other spirits in and out of embodiment and learning new spirit lessons.

A part of your consciousness can also go to the etheric realms when you are awake. Only a portion of your spiritual essence remains entirely within your body; the other aspects of it fly to destinations on planet earth and in other worlds. This investigative component of your spirit remains connected with the one residing in your body by a tiny thread of high-vibration light. This connection enables your higher consciousness to come and go at will. All the while you are unaware of its peregrinations.

Here is an example of how this process works: When I bring down material for this book and others, I sit at my computer and type the words or write them by hand on a pad of paper. My mind is aware of the content I am writing. It appears that I am the only one involved in the writing process. It also appears that the entire task is occurring in the third dimension.

But that is not the case at all.

I am, in fact, sitting at the computer typing words into its memory. My left brain is monitoring the sentence structures I am creating and noticing the typographical errors and tracking the logic of the material. But I am not writing it.

My higher consciousness is tapping into a dimension that vibrates at a very high frequency. The spirit who was my father in my current lifetime is there with me, but he is also traversing multiple dimensions beyond the one where my consciousness has traveled. My father sends telepathic thoughts from those distant realms to my higher consciousness, which forwards them to my body consciousness, which captures and documents them in the third dimension.

On the one hand, I feel similar to the way I always do. I am working at the computer. I am aware of what time it is and how tired I am. I get hungry and hear the telephone ring. On the other hand, I know that these words are not being produced by my left brain. I am not formulating rational thoughts with linear connections. I am not editing and rewriting as I go. I am simply sitting and typing. The results are page after page of prose communicating content that I can barely remember. When I review the material afterward, it is as if I am reading someone else's writing for the first time. In many ways, that is what I am doing.

This book describes the reality of the higher realms, which transcends the limits of time and space, and explains how you can apply principles from that reality in your life right now in the third dimension. It gives you access to wisdom that may heretofore have been unavailable to you. May these provocative messages from spirit help you anticipate and understand your flights to the higher realms.

GATEWAYS

We come to you in light and love, and in remembrance of things past and future that meld into the present. We anticipate with gratitude the completion of this book, which is simultaneous with its having begun to be written.

Gateways or portals exist between the numerous higher dimensions of the spiritual realms. Even though you are in human embodiment in the third dimension, you can access those realities. This opportunity is available to you not because of your physical capability, but because of your spiritual development. The more adept you become on the path to spirit, the more easily you will be able to move between the dimensions.

These gateways are not physical structures or way stations with crossing guards. Rather, they are points of vibrational shift. Entry is restricted to those souls that can adapt their vibrational and energetic capacity significantly from one level to another.

How do you train to be able to go through these gateways? It is not something you can accomplish at the gym or by doing massive amounts of intellectual research. It comes instead with your ability to love unconditionally. This requires you to forgive the greatest trespasses, heal the deepest wounds, accept the most egregiously unacceptable transgressions and care with the most subtle gentleness of heart. It requires you to have faith in spirit when there is no reason to believe—when, if anything, there appears to be evidence all around you that God could not possibly exist at all. It demands that you be tested and then tested again, each time finding your own way with your openness to the love and guidance that is available to you from spirit.

It requires you to be detached from ever achieving the ability to navigate through the very gateways that you would like so much to enter.

How can you be ardent and detached at the same time? That is the fundamental paradox of the spiritual journey. You must be committed with every cell of your being—every corner of your consciousness—to pursuing the path of spirit with vigor and righteousness. You must also let go of the need for affirmation that you are making progress on your journey. If you need such accolades, that is your ego talking—not your higher self. And as long as your ego's insufficiencies are demanding to be met, you most certainly will not make much progress.

The gateways are accessible to those whose purpose is not to go through them, but to live every moment of every day with compassion and humanity. By not desiring to achieve anything beyond loving, you will find that the greatest achievements will come to you. You will gain entrance to the gateways of higher and higher realms, penetrating them with your love and light.

CHANNEL

Although you travel between the third dimension and the higher realities, you are not adept at recognizing when you are in your body and when you are not. We offer these hints to help you navigate the waters of the channel between the two.

When you are totally in your body, you remain linear in your thought processes and rational in your memory. You do not daydream; you do not visualize; and you certainly do not meditate. You live in your left brain, which is where your absolute body consciousness dwells.

When you undertake swimming the channel between embodiment and disembodiment, you begin to focus your attention beyond yourself. Perhaps you contemplate a potentiality. Maybe you create with artistry. Whatever your mind grasps hold of and wherever it goes, it is more patterned and less linear, more metaphoric and less literal. Poetry is to narrative what moving out of your body is to staying within it.

When you go further out, you begin to lose the sensation of causality, replacing it with connectivity. You perceive the interconnectedness of all of life through the fluid time-space continuum. You experience the future as being every bit as real as the past and the present. You sense spirits around you and intercept their telepathic messages. You are less concerned about your physical security than you are about your progress toward enlightenment.

When you are as far beyond your body as you can go without experiencing physical death, you float in the nothingness of eternity. Your dreams are more real than your daily life. Your love is unconditional; your knowing is limitless. You communicate openly and without hesitation with the spirits who surround you. You find your home where your soul resides. You care beyond caring and love beyond loving. You are at peace and not at all invested in being at peace. You are without attachments.

You are metaphor and symbol; dragon and dragonfly; beauty and beast; caricature and character; marble and memory. You are infinite.

During these moments, which usually occur when you are most free during your deepest sleep, you reaffirm your spirit links and your soul connections. You exercise your field of vision that spans lifetimes and universes. You travel faster than the speed of light to places beyond your manifest imagining. You commune with angelic presences and meet with loved ones long gone. You fill yourself with joy and sublime serenity. You create a calm center within to carry you through the turbulence without.

You give and receive the bounty of love.

TIMING

This series of messages will reframe your sense of time and space. It is intended to open the door of your higher consciousness to realms beyond what you can see with your eyes and touch with your fingers. We give you these gifts of insight because we trust that they will be used appropriately by those who can benefit from them.

Timing is a key consideration of your life in human embodiment. You act when you believe that the support for your actions will be the strongest and the resistance to them will have the least influence. You factor in others' willingness to help you achieve your desired ends; you try to avoid as many obstacles as you can, preferring instead an uncluttered path.

That is good.

But however well modulated and calibrated your timing may be, it is irrelevant once you leave the third dimension because it does not exist in the higher realms. And if it does not exist, it cannot have any impact on you.

You believe, for instance, that there are moments when the spirits gather around you, and you take pen in hand to write the messages they send to you. You frame the higher dimensions to mimic your physical reality. You think that the spirits arrive, talk with and through your father to you, and then you record what they have to say. You see this channeling as a linear, time-bound process. In the morning you have a blank pad of paper and a pen full of ink. By afternoon that paper has words you have written on it by hand. By evening those words have been typed into your computer and printed out onto a page.

It is obvious, isn't it, that the material you read on the pages of text at the end of the day did not exist at the beginning of the day?

No, it isn't obvious at all. In fact, the opposite is true.

In the higher dimensions those pages of text already exist, and your books already exist. The spirits have already visited you enough times to have communicated this new collection of messages. You have already autographed copies of the books that, from your perspective in the third dimension, you haven't even written yet.

This is a strange concept for you to grasp—one so extraordinary that we will spend this entire book explaining it and offering examples of it. But for now, understand that what you call timing is not as critical as you believe it is. More central is your commitment to doing the work of spirit. This guides to you carve out time to take pen in hand and write the messages. Your timing is always impeccable because we can show up at any time, which for us is not at any particular time at all.

REMEMBERING

The process of being in human embodiment is that of remembering what you already know. In the time-space continuum that exists in other dimensions, your current and future reality on earth is synonymous with your past. Time-based distinctions do not exist.

Thus life is as much about remembering—even if it relates to what you label your future—as it is about discovering. Yes, you do make up your life as you go along. You also remember it while it is unfolding before you as if it has already occurred.

You may have trouble grasping this idea. Third-dimensional assumptions limit your ability to release your rigid demarcations between past, present and future. So you must take what we say as an article of faith.

Then again, perhaps it need not be an article of faith at all. Let's say that you are looking for a new home to purchase. You tour a number of them, all of which do not seem quite right. Then you walk into one, and it immediately feels like home to you. You are certain that you would be happy there. You spontaneously envision a deck spilling over with lush plants in clay pots. You imagine a new rug in the living room and different colors on the walls.

You have just remembered your future in that house. You have transcended your physical reality and accessed your future as if it were already accomplished. In truth, it does already exist in the higher dimensions. All that is left to be done is the accomplishment of the steps that link the present condition of the house with the future state of the house.

As you buy the terra-cotta pots and plant the flowers, select the carpet and paint the walls, you believe that you are simply acting on your initial inspiration. But what you are actually doing is manifesting what already exists beyond the third dimension. You are creating an eventuality—not acting on a potentiality.

This remembering is a function of free will. Nothing requires you to take the steps that construct what you saw when you first entered the house. You can do nothing or go in the opposite direction. Your free will is the engine of your karmic evolution. It keeps you from being a slave to your memories of the future.

Nonetheless, you will have a tendency to assimilate your future remembrances into your present actions. There are many catalysts for such actions, not the least of which is the alignment of your higher consciousness with the reality that exists beyond the third dimension. Your soul lives in those planes.

It prefers congruence with the results of its time travel there. The more conscious you are, the more adept you will be at bridging your current reality with your memories of the future with grace and fluidity.

FORGETTING

Just as you can remember the future when you enter the higher dimensions, so can you forget the past. The past as you know it in your material world does not disappear. Rather, what occurred recedes into the background until it becomes irrelevant.

You would gladly forget your most painful moments and humiliating encounters if you could. Despite that desire, they are often the most difficult ones to lay to rest because they have wounded you so deeply. There is little to be done after-the-fact to reverse what occurred, although with significant intervention it is possible. This occurs rarely because such intervention is hardly ever warranted. And even when it is, neither we nor you are at liberty to change the course of karma through such intercessions.

What can you do to forget what you wish had never occurred at all? First, you can stop blaming yourself or anyone else for the fact that the incident happened. Blame only compounds the suffering; it does nothing to lessen it. After you have ceased the cycle of blaming, start the cycle of forgiving. Whenever you remember what happened, instead of dwelling on it, choose to forgive, forgive, forgive. Within the parameters of the third dimension, that is the quickest and most effective route to forgetting.

But there is more that you can do as well. You can commit to completing your karma regarding the incident or the relationship as resourcefully as you can. This requires you to consider all of the ways you are still hanging on to the experience, then let them all go. It calls on you to refrain from assuming that something similar will occur again and instead anticipate its opposite.

Finally, you must consciously embody spirit every time you remember the event. Stop whatever you are doing. Open your heart and fill it with light. Count your blessings. Make additional space for the power of the divine to pulsate in every cell of your being. When you do that, you have essentially forgotten what was bothering you so.

As you move toward such karmic completion, you also enable the impressions from the experience to weaken and then vanish from your soul. At that point your soul no longer carries the burden of these memories within it, and you no longer have the responsibility of doing what it takes to cleanse them. When your soul is clear, it has then forgotten that the experience ever occurred. With a lighter load, you move more smoothly on the path of spiritual evolution. You have forgotten something from the past that once held you back. The horizon ahead shines with brilliant opportunity.

You are then free again to remember the future.

DOGMA

Dogma consists of prescriptions about what to believe, how to behave and where to go for comfort and security (which is usually outside of yourself). Dogmas may seem relatively harmless to you despite the fact that you cannot and will not fit into their frameworks. Your attitude might be, if others choose to live according to a dogma, that is their option. But you choose not to do so. You know what you believe, and you follow it to the best of your ability. You do not press it onto others.

Such a laissez-faire approach is in keeping with the path of non-judging and is entirely appropriate. However, it is in the nature of dogma not to stop at requiring its adherents to live according to it. Dogma demands that the circle of adherents grow until it encompasses all of humanity. This means bringing people into the fold who are willing to be led there and discrediting—or even killing—those who refuse to do so.

How do you respond to such dogmatic demands without becoming dogmatic yourself? That is a hefty responsibility as long as you are in the third dimension. It is not so difficult once you leave it, however, for dogmas cannot exist in the higher dimensions. A dogma is an entirely human dynamic embedded in your materially based way of interacting with and attempting to control each other.

Imagine that someone comes to you with a dogma that you refuse to accept. What is the most effective way to respond? You must love that person, dogma and all. But you must also separate yourself from that person's karmic path. If you engage in a battle of wits with that individual, you will become involved in a win-lose war of the mind and the will, if not also the body. There is nothing holy about any of those wars, no matter how apparently sacred their purpose.

Love and then detach. That is the appropriate third-dimensional response.

But you also have options beyond the third dimension. You can place the tenets of that dogma in the archives that exist in a timeless future, evidence of a phase in the spiritual evolution of masses of people on earth. The dogma does exist now in the material world of the millennial anniversary of the planet. And it also exists in the archives of the higher dimensions that transcend the world as you know it.

Treat such dogma as a fascinating, informative artifact of a slice in time rather than an immediate threat to your freedom of thought. You will have more impact in neutralizing its influence that way than you will in trying to extinguish it head-on in a battle between dogmas in which there can ultimately be no victor.

DISTANCE

You measure distance in terms of the linear—or curvilinear—space between one point and another. In the third dimension such measures are helpful in organizing your lives. When you know how far away something is, you can more easily calculate how long it will take to get there. When you know how big something is (the distance from one side of its mass to another) you know how much space it will take up in a room or on a piece of land.

Distance is an important factor in the third dimension because materiality influences everything that happens there. Your world revolves around moving dense masses of atoms and cells from one place to another. But when you transcend the material world, distance becomes irrelevant.

Imagine, then, what a reality would be like if it did not require the transportation of a mass between physical locations. What if being were entirely energetic instead of physical? What if, within that energy-based reality, whenever you wanted to move from one place to another, you could accomplish that with a mere thought? What if it were not necessary to move anything because there were nothing physical to move?

Distance in the higher dimensions does not exist in the same way that you know it. It takes on a whole new meaning in the spiritual realms. Distance there is the space between the potential of having a thought and the thought itself. Distance becomes, then, the difference between a potentiality and its manifestation.

We will talk a great deal about this concept throughout the messages contained in this book. If you are to access the intelligence and wisdom inherent in the higher dimensions, you must become more conversant about and comfortable with distance as it is measured magnetically rather than in terms of linear mass.

BORDERS

You create borders around physical space on the planet in order to establish lines of demarcation between one area and another. You buy a piece of land, register the title to the property with the appropriate record-keepers, erect a fence around it and call it yours. The borders enable you to know what belongs to you and what belongs to another.

Borders in the material world function mostly to establish ownership. A border between one country and another indicates where the land belonging to one country stops and where the land belonging to another country begins. Within those borders are rules and regulations about how people living on that geopolitical land mass called a country will coexist.

Borders help organize how you live, but they do so through ownership distinctions and the privileges inherent in such. This organization is not based on unity and oneness. Rather, its foundation is separation and possession. Ownership enables people to say, "This is mine, and that is yours." But the dynamic does not stop there. The game becomes, "I will try to obtain what you have through either persuasion or purchase or power." To own something is to desire to own more, then even more.

So borders set up boundaries that invite crossing as much as they establish checkpoints. This manifests as, "I am here, but I want to be there. What will it take to penetrate the border between the two?" or "I have this, but I want that. What is required to obtain it?"

In the higher dimensions there is no ownership because there is nothing to own. There are no borders because there is nothing to divide up. Without borders there is no need to try to acquire something you do not have or to go somewhere you cannot go. Nothing is unobtainable because there is nothing to obtain.

So the dynamics of interaction on the higher planes revolve around being rather than doing or having. They focus on the evolution of the soul, the attainment of higher and still higher vibratory capacities, the drive to merge with the One. They assume absolute interconnectedness in a borderless world.

DISCREPANCY

The time-space distinctions through which you manage your life enable you to determine discrepancies between what you say might occur and what actually happens. For instance, you might commit to arriving at a distant location at 7:00 and then not get there until 7:30. That represents a measurable discrepancy between your promise and the result.

Space-based discrepancies are also measurable. You might be told that an office is 16 feet by $20\frac{1}{2}$ feet in size. But upon measuring it, you discover that it is actually $15\frac{1}{2}$ feet by $20\frac{1}{2}$ feet. That represents a measurable discrepancy that can be easily determined and verified.

Much of your daily activity is directed at removing the discrepancies in your life so that it can be more precise and predictable. You want a car with zero defects because it will be more reliable. You want to schedule meetings with people who are prompt so that you can avoid running late yourself. Being able to plan ahead or trust the durability of something adds to the quality of your life.

In the higher dimensions no such discrepancies can be determined. It is not necessary to plan, since things occur simultaneously instead of sequentially. In fact, it is impossible to plan under such conditions. It is not necessary to assure the reliability of a product because there are no material things to keep in good repair. And as far as a promise goes, on the higher planes intention is synonymous with action. Whatever you promise will be accomplished in the same moment.

What is it like to exist in a world that is free of discrepancies? You are liberated from the need to address them, which then releases you to live entirely in the moment. You embody all that is, simultaneously. You discover instantly, move effortlessly, and engage in multiple conversations at once. When discrepancies are not a factor in your existence, you no longer have to allow for all of the "what ifs" that consume so much of your time, energy and resources in the third dimension. There is no need to do contingency planning because there are no contingencies, which at their root are collections of responses anticipating discrepancies.

MARGINS

Your redefinition of margins will help you understand the process that guides you from one dimension to
the other. At the margins of the third dimension are areas
of gravitational force, which is a form of magnetic energy,
that pull you toward that energy field. Counter to those
are pockets of force that pull you away from the third
dimension and out into higher vibrational realities.

These forces look like your mountain ranges, rising
high then dropping into deep valleys. The pattern of
energy shifts up and down based on the movement
within the earth immediately below that geographic
point. That movement is constantly changing the magnetics of the planet. As a result, the margins between the
third and fourth dimension are undergoing continual
flux. There is no singular, predictable passageway to take
you from one dimension to the other because the margins between the two are ebbing and flowing like the
ocean, every moment of every day.

So the margins are not like your third-dimensional
ones, where you can take a material object and identify

or create an area close to its periphery that can remain labeled, identifiable and constant. Rather, these margins experience huge vacillations, energy vortices and eruptions, swirls and cascades. They also manifest as placid pools. This is a living margin, not a static one.

The magnetics surrounding the planet are shifting in a transformative way for a reason that is both linked with the inner movements of the earth's core and independent of them. It is independent of the earth's core because of the influence of the spiritual transcendence of a critical mass of people living on the planet at this moment in time. As each of you becomes liberated from your karmic burdens and moves closer to spirit, your being begins to vibrate more harmoniously with the higher dimensions. You emanate light and love to a far greater degree. And because all of reality is interconnected, those emanations influence the vibratory mantle around the planet.

When enough of you are more closely aligned with spirit, the magnetic structure of the planet can change. We have determined that such a potentiality has in fact become a reality. Nonetheless, throughout the planet you are struggling with the forces of darkness which, like the strongest gravitational pulls imaginable, are pressuring many to resist this global transcendence.

Thus the planetary magnetics are experiencing enormous volatility. We watch tidal waves of ebb and flow occur daily in some geographic locations. Other places are more stable. Create your own inner calm when you begin to feel the fear-based instability that surrounds you. Go deep within to find your source. Love all. And do not hesitate to traverse the margins, even if they seem more like minefields than garden paths.

DEATH

When your soul leaves your physical body upon death, you become liberated from the gravitational pull of the third dimension. At that point the margins we have just described become irrelevant.

Your body is what keeps you tied to the third dimension. When your soul is no longer residing in that cellular mass, it is immediately released into the higher planes, where the predominance of material form is replaced by the predominance of vibrational magnetics.

What is it like to move so swiftly, and at times abruptly, from one form of existence to another? Think of it as having been released from bondage. In this case the bondage is your physical body and the material circumstances in which it has dwelled. It is similar in structure—if not intention—to the imprisonment of the body in a jail cell or the control of the mind with onslaughts of biased information. When you undergo physical death, your soul is set free from its temporary residence in the body you created and chose to occupy during the lifetime just completed.

When you die you realize that you are going home. Whereas during your lifetime on the planet you may have thought that the third dimension was your home, you recognize the instant of your death that it was in fact more like a hotel—a way station for the spiritual traveler. Granted, it was a beautiful home-away-from-home. And it enabled you to encounter many fellow travelers with whom you could work and play, explore and grow. But it was more like a ceaseless transition than a destination.

You understand that truth when you leave your body upon death.

You are welcomed home by souls you have known for millennia—ones who have shared earthly lifetimes with you and others whom you have known solely in the higher dimensions. They await you, ready to celebrate the progress you made during your most recent lifetime and to help you define your next steps in the etheric realms.

There is work to do on the other side, but only after you have reviewed the lifetime you just completed. You must identify the ways in which you moved closer to spirit and, at the other end of the continuum, the catalysts for your regression into darkness.

Death is a joyful occasion. It commemorates returning and rebirth. Remember that whenever you contemplate your own death. Imagine the rush of love that you will feel when you know that you are on your way home. Yes, you will grieve the temporary loss of your ability to relate to others in an earthly way. But you will still be in their lives, both while they remain on the planet and when they, too, leave it.

CHOICE

Your definition of choice assumes that the alternatives worth considering can be made apparent to you. You believe that it is possible to identify your options, then move ahead with a thoughtful decision-making process involving the assessment of each option and the selection of the "best" one. That is the most logical approach, it seems.

In your third-dimensional reality that may be the case. But you have many choices that transcend your material definition of the here and now. For instance, you may be trying to decide whether you will take a vacation to Greece. On the surface the decision may appear to be guided by a series of obvious considerations:

- Do you have the time to go?
- Do you have the money to go?
- Is that where you want to be for ten days?
- Why would you choose Greece over other destination spots?

You ponder these questions, then decide whether to take the trip.

But there are other less apparent questions that also deserve consideration:

- ♦ What kind of soul memory might you have about past lives in Greece?
- ♦ Are you being drawn there to rediscover or renew, complete or heal?
- ♦ What might you be resisting if you do not go? What opportunity might you miss?
- ♦ What is your intention in visiting that country?
- ♦ What is your intuition telling you about the trip?

Every choice you make affects multiple levels of your reality. Often the most tangible outcomes are the least relevant. What you do with your time and how you spend your money may be far less important than the effect of transporting yourself to a geographic location where you have walked before. Every choice is both a life decision and a soul decision. The latter is far less evident than the former.

So we move to the question of how you can make any choice at all—and on what basis—if so much information is hidden from you. Isn't it difficult to make worthwhile choices under such circumstances? No, it is not.

We are not advocating that you cease your attempts to make good decisions based on your immediate material circumstances. Nor do we believe that it is best for you to become so preoccupied with discovering the hidden meaning in everything that you become paralyzed into inaction. But we do believe that it is worth your considering additional insights or intuitive senses that you might have regarding the choices you make.

You may be going to Greece because it is a lovely

vacation spot. Or you may be going because you are ready to awaken your cellular memory of having lived there centuries ago. There is the choice before you and, perhaps, the additional implications of that choice. Remain open to both. You never know what new facets of your being you will uncover along the way.

ANTICIPATION

At times you have a sense that a breakthrough is about to occur. Yet you know neither its catalyst nor its source. This vague awareness has you jumpy—and more impatient than usual. It is as if you want to speed up time, to fast-forward to the future. You anticipate something welcome on the horizon, yet you cannot identify exactly what it could be.

Quiet yourself for a moment and experience what is occurring within your body. You feel your energy pulsating within. It is more insistent, as if your cells want you to run forward—to fly instantaneously into a reality yet to come—even when your body is still.

What are your options? Let's observe what is before you.

+ You can make peace with your condition of not knowing and become comfortable with the unfolding you are experiencing both internally and externally.

+ You can cognitively try to determine what is ahead. That will yield limited results, since your rational mind is sorely inadequate when it comes to accessing the higher planes, where some of your anticipations live.

♦ You can relax into the anticipations and let them take you wherever they might. You must approach this process, if you choose to pursue it, with a complete lack of preferences and a profound openness to what you might observe and experience. Embark on a journey with no purpose but to see where it leads.

If you select the last option, we suggest that you:

♦ Quiet your body and your mind. Go deep into a state of relaxation. Move to the void. Occupy the place of nothingness.

♦ Ask your higher consciousness what is waiting to be revealed to you. Then wait for the answer. It may arrive in the form of a vision, words, a bodily sensation. When it begins to present itself, allow it to flow over you and into you. Breathe with it. Welcome it, but do not own it.

♦ Open your heart to the love vibration that accompanies this message, whatever form it takes. Be at one with the information that is coming through you. Allow it to be your reality. See what additional doors it opens, what new paths it paves for you. Then go through those doors; follow those paths.

♦ Become fully present in that altered reality. Move with it, breathe with it, pulsate with it. You have nothing to fear; no harm can come to you. See with open/closed eyes; touch with your inner senses; hear with your heart.

When you are ready to return to your earthly and

bodily reality, remain a moment longer in gratitude for the insight that has been granted you. Know that you have just been blessed with the wisdom of a higher order of knowing. Then bring that into the physical plane and integrate it into your existence in the current time and place.

FORCE

Your context for the use of force is that its purpose is to compel and control, repel and resist. A force, you believe, exerts itself in a particular direction, creating the movement (whether it involves objects or ideas) from one location or state of mind to another. Force stimulates change where it otherwise might not occur.

That is an accurate portrayal of force as it exists in the third dimension. But what happens in the higher realities? How does force manifest? What are its effects?

When you move beyond the physical plane, force becomes more closely linked with visions, thoughts and feelings than it is with physical actions. As you transcend the limitations of dense matter, you find that your thoughts, for instance, carry a great deal more force than they did on the earthly plane. In the higher realms you might think something and then become immediately aware of its manifesting somewhere, even if it is not directly before you.

In the spiritual realms there is an almost instantaneous feedback loop between your mental images, perceptions and emotions and their effect. Such circumstances invite abuse as well as respect. Beings in the higher dimensions must surround themselves with impenetrable light aligned with the love vibration; they must embody spirit at all times, lest they fuel its absence.

So force in the higher realms is inherent in every momentary outburst or sequestered impression because the vibratory environment is so sensitive and responsive. Physical matter vibrates at a much slower rate and is thus less responsive to forces that are not physical (although through psychokinesis people can move objects with their thoughts, and most certainly spiritual entities can influence physical matter with their energies).

Nonetheless, we caution you not to assume that because you do not experience the immediate repercussions of your thoughts, feelings, visions and words in your immediate external environment, they have no influence. Quite the contrary is true. In fact, they have the same impact in the higher realms that we just described. The difference is that you do not consciously experience this impact because you are not aware of the extent to which you dwell in those planes.

Remember that all of creation is interconnected. The force of your thoughts, words and deeds influences all of the universes as well as the reality directly in front of you. You may think that you cannot move a mountain with a memory or fan a flame with a fantasy, but quite the opposite is true.

Acknowledge the force inherent in everything you do and all that you are. Keep spirit uppermost in your head and your heart. That way the force you exert will be aligned with your higher purpose—and all creation.

REALITIES

Commentary about your life is irrelevant outside of the context of the larger field in which it is being played out. Nonetheless, you see what is immediately before you and treat it as your reality. How can you not, when it is so palpable and ever present?

And yet, you also move in and out of the higher dimensions with greater ease. That could represent reality to you as well. But it does not. Why not?

The answers are numerous. But the central one is that you continue to place your body consciousness ahead of the other ways in which you could perceive the dynamics of your existence. You are uncomfortable with the huge change a shift from that perspective would introduce. You welcome new perspectives, and yet you can go only so far in adopting them.

Understand that to live in two realities requires you to refrain from having a preference of one over the other. You must travel between the two of them not whenever you wish, but whenever it serves you most in mission and lesson. You must transcend your tendency to want to

38

control your perceptual antennae based on what is most convenient for you. Your life and your path are not about convenience; they are about effectiveness.

What does it take for you to be effective?

First, you must joyfully embrace your full capabilities. Think about the implications of this declaration. Your ability to traverse multiple dimensions need not be a burden or even a responsibility. Rather, it is a gift to be accepted with grace and joy. You deserve this gift; you also arranged to be able to receive and apply it in this lifetime. To deny an aspect of it or to begrudge the fact that it has become a central aspect of your life is to denigrate one of the greatest blessings anyone could have.

Next, take care to use these abilities appropriately. When you came into this embodiment, you committed to one of the most important missions you have ever tried to achieve. This capability is critical to your success. It is not frivolous; it is not redundant or unnecessary; it is not negotiable. You have it. You must also use it wisely. Only when you have lived up to your highest potential can you relax your focus on the cause you are pursuing.

And finally, your intentions must remain honorable and uncorrupted, no matter how tempting the offers might be to use your power for ill-advised ends. You are worthy of our respect, but you must also continue to earn it. We will never withhold it, but your actions can diminish its light-force.

PERMANENT

You long for permanence amidst the tumult of change. You look around you and see lives that appear to be tossed about by the vagaries of life as it unfolds day after day, year after year. When you desire permanence, it is an indicator that you have lost sight of the most permanent aspect of your existence.

And what is that? It is your soul, which has existed throughout millennia—so many millennia, in fact, that to your soul a century encompasses only a tiny imprint of time. You as a soul entity have existed longer than you can fathom and will continue to exist even longer than that. Your soul has pulsated in its beingness so long as to be almost without birth. And it will continue to pulsate in its beingness so much longer as to be almost without death.

To be almost without birth and death is, at its most fundamental, to be permanent. Your soul—your very essence—is distinctive in its uniqueness within the context of its permanence. It is unique in that no other soul in existence carries the imprints that yours does. No

other being in or out of embodiment walks the same path that you do or has the same opportunities for karmic healing and completion that you do. Within that extraordinary uniqueness is your everlasting soul life—the cosmic dance that you enact throughout and beyond time and space.

The permanence of your soul is assured. The impermanence of your existence on the earth plane is also assured. You have been born many times into human embodiment. You have died many times and been released from human embodiment. The cycle of your existence as a human being has been repeated over and over again. Beginnings have been followed by intermediary steps, which led eventually to endings. That is the human condition—and a condition of the physical world.

Nonetheless, all of life is spirit, and spirit never ceases to exist. It simply transforms into different vessels or venues. So the permanence of spirit in all that is remains assured, as does the permanence of your soul.

You are spirit in the flesh. You are also spirit when you leave the flesh of your body behind upon death. At that point your spirit merges more completely with your soul and takes up residence in the more etheric higher dimensions. Your soul lives on; your spirit lives on. Your life essence remains vibrant and vital, regardless of the domain in which it resides.

That, then, is permanence. To want your transitory life in a transient material world to afford you permanence is to ask for the impossible—and to dishonor the blessing of permanence that is yours without asking.

LIFETIME

You have a clear idea of the prior lifetimes that most influence your actions in this one. They carry similar themes and patterns. They speak to your deepest beliefs and most heartfelt commitments. They offer you guideposts based on universal wisdom and boundaryless knowing. Your former embodiments help frame your current options and opportunities.

But if you believe that this lifetime is constituted like all of your others, you are mistaken. For this lifetime affords you a chance to transcend all of the limitations that held you back previously. Inherent in this embodiment is an accessibility to spirit that has been unavailable since the days of Atlantis. Yes, this is another in a long series of lifetimes. But it is like no other.

On the one hand, this embodiment appears to be bounded in the same way that all of your others have been. You were born; you are making your way. You struggle, you hope, you work, you rejoice. You feel humble, you are proud. You experience pain; you know the source of meaning.

On the other hand, all of these experiences are occurring in a context that is unbounded. For you now have the ability to approach the higher dimensions in a way that was previously closed off to you. This is a bounded lifetime lived in a larger field of unboundedness.

Which reality is prevalent—boundedness or unboundedness? That question has no answer because it is a function of whichever one you choose. If you focus on your third-dimensional challenges and conquests, it will be a bounded lifetime. If your world encompasses the higher vibratory energies that exist beyond this planetary home, it will be an unbounded lifetime. Both are equally available to you. We can inform and guide you, but we cannot create your preferences or make your choices for you.

What does it mean to live an unbounded lifetime? Isn't that an oxymoron? After all, you still must accept one boundary, and that is death itself. You cannot escape that one, or wish it out of existence.

That is true. But before your soul leaves your body this time, you can live as much in the higher dimensions as you do in the third dimension. You can perceive what is occurring within and around you from a place of deeper knowing rather than relying on the limited lenses of your immediate reality. You can release your assumptions about your abilities and potentialities, then leap into the unfathomable future that coexists with your emergent past. You can see life as fluid and embryonic, transformative and translucent, precarious and propelled, momentous and momentary, fragile and forever.

It is all of these and none of these. In its unbounded abundance, your lifetime is finally free.

DORMANCY

In winter many plants lie dormant. Their vital processes slow down to an almost imperceptible pace, but they do not cease. This dormancy enables life to continue with the lowest possible expenditure of essential energy, which is in short supply.

As human beings you do not consider yourselves as experiencing dormancy in any form. Yet you do have such phases built into the evolution of your soul. They occur when you are in embodiment and when you are not.

Consider this. Your soul is growing in its capacity to encompass spirit. It is moving toward spirit as you evolve into your existence in higher and higher dimensions. This can be accelerated by your intention to embody light and your attention to being love throughout every moment of every day.

Such commitment is difficult to maintain month after month, year after year, lifetime after lifetime. Times of dormancy are sometimes necessary so you can carry on with greater force and effectiveness at other moments in your soul's journey.

You may think that your spirit is experiencing a temporary dormancy when you sleep. But that is not the case at all. In fact, it is far more active during the hours you spend in deep sleep than it is during the day. Why is that so? When you are awake, you become preoccupied with third-dimensional cares and concerns, many of which draw you away from spirit. These distractions are not necessarily a waste of time, but they do cause you to be less aligned with spirit.

Your spiritual dormancy is something different from sleep, however. It is not just a temporary movement of your attention away from the One. It is a period of rest and respite from your spiritual work. It is rather like a sabbatical from your spiritual path.

These moments occur usually when you are out of embodiment, often just after you have completed a lifetime and are in need of soul-rejuvenating rest. You can choose to go into dormancy for a while with the foreknowledge that when you return to active consciousness you will once again pursue your journey to the One.

In dormancy you are neither awake nor asleep. You are suspended in time and space, cradled by spirit.

BETWEEN

In your third-dimensional reality you have many occasions when you are between one place or object and another. This betweenness can be time-based (between 2PM and 3PM) or space-based (between Pine and Bush Streets).

The word *between* expresses the relationship of elements along a continuum of reality. Their juxtaposition can be identified and determined by their separateness. If there were no distinction between one hour and another, one location and another, one person and another, "between" could not exist.

In the higher dimensions the sense of betweenness becomes almost imperceptible. Spiritual entities vibrate with such high frequencies, their attunement enables the unification of their thought patterns into oneness of focus and force. Fragmentation of thought is far more rare than what you experience on earth. Communication is vibratory—not word-based. It is also instantaneous. Thus the sense of betweenness disappears in a field of alignment and unity.

You are accustomed to traversing distances of in-betweenness, whether you are flying in an airplane from New York to New Delhi or planning an event that will occur three months from now. These distances are not problematic, really. They give you the opportunity to leave one reality behind and prepare for the one you anticipate in the future.

Such transitions are not necessary when you leave the third dimension. You realize that your spirit can travel from New York to New Delhi in a nanosecond. In fact, you can be in both places at once. You recognize that you can experience an event while you are planning it. You discover that you converse with another best when you are both communicating simultaneously—not sequentially. The more you remove the in-betweenness, the more effective you become.

What if you did that on earth? What if you understood that you are indeed in Kansas City and Kosovo at the same time? What if you realized that whatever you envision is already a reality? What if you knew that you communicated with others with your thoughts and feelings as much as with your words and actions?

That is already true, you know. There is no in-betweenness. You simply have not realized it yet.

OVERSOUL

The divine oversoul is alive within and around you. You are transformed by its power every time you choose to love rather than hate, to forgive rather than judge, to be guided by faith rather than fear. Even when you succumb to judging and fear, the oversoul lives within you.

What is the difference between your soul and the divine oversoul? Your soul is the vessel for your karmic patterns as they impact your spiritual evolution. It is unique to you, reflecting the changes that occur as a result of your decisions and actions, both in the third dimension and beyond it. It is never static. With every breath you take and every thought you think, your soul shifts and stretches, shrinks and stabilizes.

The divine oversoul, on the other hand, is the God-force as it exists within all of creation and apart from all of creation. The divine oversoul is all that you are and are becoming. It is also far beyond what you are or ever could be at this point in your spiritual evolution. It is the destination you are striving to reach and each step that you take to reach it.

It is father and mother, self and other, being and non-being, all and nothingness. It is womb and world. It is eternal life and omnipresent, inexhaustible love. It changes with every soul-shift you make and yet remains unchanged.

You merge with the divine oversoul when you leave your physical body upon death. You return to a place of all-consuming love and light. But you remain there only for a moment. For you must continue on your soul's progress to higher and higher realms, deeper and deeper love, fewer and fewer attachments.

You become one with the oversoul and are at the same time apart from it. It is home and way station, challenge and completion. All of your soul selves from your multiple embodiments integrate within the energetic field of the oversoul, yet they remain distinct from it until the karmic residue they carry has been cleansed and healed.

Embrace the accessible inaccessible oversoul. It is spirit unadulterated yet able to thrive within your adulterated being.

DISCONTENT

You expect that as you move closer to spirit—as you become more adept at accessing higher and higher dimensions—you will live in bliss. Instead, you experience a new source of torment caused by your inability to relate to others the way you used to. This disturbs you and causes consternation. You know not what to make of these alien feelings that are at once fulfilling and frustrating.

Do not be alarmed if your third-dimensional discontent grows in proportion with your contentment in the higher dimensions. It is a predictable, natural reaction requiring modifications in the cues and clues you use to determine your effectiveness.

Let us explain.

Typically when you are interacting with others, you feel you are making a difference if you are helping them address issues immediately before them with greater insight and acuity. They give you positive feedback when they experience progress—when an obstacle before them has been moved or removed. You see the change; they see the change. You both recognize the progress. That is gratifying.

But when you begin to move more adroitly into and throughout the higher dimensions, you lose your ability to exist so completely in the third dimension. The obstacles that people face seem irrelevant to you. Their attachments seem nonessential. Their worries appear to be unfounded. You have difficulty relating to them from their materially based frame of reference. You feel yourself becoming disengaged during conversations or avoiding any contact with people at all.

You begin to experience your apparent ineffectiveness. You no longer invest as much in assisting others. They sense this. Some feel abandoned. Those who are more spiritually aware understand that your former way of relating to them has been replaced by a more profound—if detached—one. You see the bigger picture, the broader patterns, the larger implications. You communicate those; you honor the spiritual existence and essence of the other person in doing so.

Do not allow yourself to be tormented by the demands and expectations of those who remain firmly rooted in the third dimension. They are who they are, where they are. You have moved beyond their circumstances. Attempting to remain there with them will hold you back and unnecessarily limit your progress.

Love them. Bring them into your light. But do not live in theirs.

ESSENCE

Your essence is that of the divine. It surrounds you like a vibratory cloak, shimmering and sparkling in the glorious colors of the spectrum. We see your essence more than your physical body when we work with you. We merge with your essence when we want to alert you to our presence. We heal your physical body by first realigning your essence.

What is this essence? It is the vibratory zone that provides the transition between your physical body and your etheric existence. It is the source of your inspiration, the channel for your communion with spirit. It provides strength and stability despite your enervating, chaotic daily life. It helps you find a clear path through the confusion and inspires you to take leaps of faith that at the time seem to be no more equivocal than a walk in the park.

The more effectively you can tap into this essence, the more easily guided your life will be. Rather than your making every choice based on rational thought and linear observation, your essence will fuel your ability to see patterns in apparent randomness. These patterns are embedded in the spiritual essence—and oneness—of all of life.

The more you can see these patterns, the more you can become at one with them. Being at one with what in the third dimension seems to be randomness, but is actually the pulsing of the life-force in the higher dimensions beyond time and space, takes you more exquisitely into the higher realms. These higher realms enable you to embody the God-force within your being.

So your essence, in fact, is not just something that surrounds your physical being. Rather, when you move into that essence, you become it and it becomes you. Your entire body vibrates with the same frequency and intensity as your essence. You then remove the physical mass that is your body and transform it into essence. You are at once alive as an individual in the third dimension and transformed into a being that is entirely spirit.

You are human; you are God. You are the essence of all that is and ever will be.

TRANSITIONS

When you begin to access the higher dimensions on a regular basis, you enter into a life dominated by transition. Rather than finding comfort in permanence and predictability, you become accustomed to movement and ambiguity. You know that you are on the path when you have lost your ability—and desire—to control your destiny. You know you have wandered off it when you find that you can plan meticulously and live out those precise plans.

You may question these statements, especially given our prior assertions that whatever you envision becomes a reality in the higher dimensions. Isn't envisioning the same as planning? Yes and no. Planning involves the framing of a desirable outcome, then the prescription of the steps necessary to get there. Envisioning involves insight into a spirit-infused future state, with no preferred methodology for getting there.

Why does this difference matter so much if the result is the same? In one case you plan how to get there. In the other you trust spirit to help you find the most appropriate process for arriving there. Either way you arrive, don't you?

No, not really. Planning requires you to concretize what is essentially inaccessible. In doing that you substantially reduce the potentiality of achieving the desired conclusion. This happens because you have defined your reality in terms of third-dimensional parameters, thus limiting the degree to which you can tap into and build upon the power of spirit.

When you envision an outcome that is aligned with love and light, then detach from the need to know how you will accomplish it, you trust the process that spirit follows in leading you there. This enables you to take quantum leaps forward, avoid detours and be sensitive to synchronicity. You project yourself into the future rather than plodding your way there. You see your immediate circumstances as transitional rather than being temporary times of change that punctuate what is otherwise stable and permanent.

This effortless, perpetual transition enables you to move freely, unencumbered by expectations of what ought to be, where you ought to go and how you ought to get there. Instead you glide, aware of nothing but the wind of spirit beneath your wings.

VELOCITY

Velocity is the speed of motion in a given direction. Speed is measured by the time it takes to traverse a certain distance. You can calculate velocity by measuring where an object began at a particular time and how long it took to transport itself or be transported to another location.

Since your physical world revolves around the production and acquisition of physical objects, much labor is invested in transporting those objects. The velocity of the transport vehicles you use has been central to your ability to manufacture more goods and distribute them faster and more broadly.

In recent years your sense of velocity has been undergoing a revolutionary change. Computers now enable you to exchange and disseminate information in the blink of an eye. Whereas not so long ago communication required in-person, telephonic or recorded contact or the writing and reading of the printed word, it can now be accomplished instantaneously. The velocity with which news is heralded globally via the Internet is unprecedented, as is the speed of your international monetary exchange, among other examples.

This velocity enables you to experience conditions that are increasingly similar to the ones that exist in the higher dimensions, where the thinking of a thought is simultaneous with its manifestation. When the space between a thought and its enactment becomes so infinitesimal as to be nonexistent, you move toward zero-based velocity. And as you approach zero-based velocity, an extraordinary shift occurs: You reverse the order in which you are accustomed to experiencing events as they unfold. The action precedes the envisioning of it—and even the decision to act.

Think of what happens in extreme crisis situations. Many people who have lived through them report that time as they typically experience it slows down. They become detached from what is happening, appearing to be more observer than participant. They act without thinking through what to do. Only later do they understand how remarkable their actions were.

The crisis has been a catalyst for their release of all third-dimensional limitations on their ability to respond. They move out of their body and into the flow of spirit. This increases the velocity of their response in relation to the speed of the material world. They adopt zero-based velocity. And thus they are saved.

LITMUS

Litmus is a chemical that measures the existence of its opposite. It reacts to a countervailing substance, providing a visible record of their having come together.

What is the litmus test for your life? What is to be measured, and how do you go about it?

You follow a path of light punctuated by darkness. So one litmus test might be the degree to which you live in the shadows. But that is not litmus, really. It is more of a calibration of shades of gray.

Remember that litmus requires one substance or reality to come into immediate contact with its opposite. The reaction between the two occurs upon contact, altering an aspect of the original substance. The ultimate litmus test of a lifetime, then, is your ability to embody pure spirit in a spirit-starved world. For when spirit deprivation comes into contact with pure spirit, it is immediately transformed.

That is the alchemy of mystical revelation and unconditional love. Whoever is loved unconditionally is forever changed by the experience. Whoever loves unconditionally is forever influenced by the experience of having done so. A revelation permanently alters one's perception of the possible. It sends a message, "I can be more than myself because I can tap into a world beyond the one I have known until now." These are the litmus tests of your journey to spirit.

The power of these litmus tests is that you cannot embellish the results. They either express the alchemy of spirit or remain ensconced in the values of mundane reality. We cannot modify the measurements or redefine the parameters. No credit is given for valid excuses or good attempts that did not hit the mark.

This litmus test exists in all dimensions, in all of the universes, throughout creation. It varies not one iota. It makes no allowances for especially troublesome circumstances or problematic threats. The standards are, in a word, standardized. They can be articulated in one multifaceted question: Whatever the situation, do you embody unconditional love? Forgive? Surrender? Accept? Have faith?

None of these conditions can be partially met. You either love unconditionally or you do not; you forgive or you do not; you surrender or you do not; you accept and have faith—or you do not.

The alchemy of the presence of pure spirit in your life transforms it. You love and forgive, surrender, accept and have faith, without question or hesitation. These acts integrate spirit into your cellular and psychic being. The reflection of this presence or absence of spirit is your life, the most discernible litmus test of all.

FRAME

These messages are being communicated to help you frame your perception of reality in radically new ways. This reframing is necessary if you are to live your daily life with greater freedom to access the higher dimensions.

Often you witness yourself and others behaving in certain ways, then you assign a cause-and-effect-based frame to what you are experiencing. This frame is rooted in third-dimensional definitions regarding the factors influencing what is occurring. You hear of someone's accidental death, for instance, and assume that it was caused by identifiable, immediate and random circumstances.

Whenever you frame your perceptions in this way, you limit your ability to see, accept and understand the larger reality in which an occurrence is implanted. At times you even actively resist acknowledging that any other forces may be at work. Instead you experience what you believe to be an injustice—the precipitous loss of life.

What if, in addition or instead, you were to frame

every occurrence from the perspective that whatever is, is perfect? Perhaps the person who died young was scheduled to leave her body precisely at that time, after having completed all of the karmic work that she came into this lifetime to accomplish. Maybe the man who loses all of his worldly belongings in an unsuccessful venture is blessed more than any other because such circumstances enable him to take greater strides in accomplishing his mission and lesson.

We see the larger realities that frame what occurs daily on the earth plane. We also recognize that much of what is obvious to us is veiled from you. Remember that everything that occurs is karmic. Understand that it is all spirit; it is also all flesh. It is both worldly and otherworldly; darkness and light; immediate and unfathomable; untimely and timeless; past, present and future occurring simultaneously.

Your frame for everything, then, needs to transcend what you see before you to embrace what you cannot see. Surrender to the unknown; trust that spirit is inherent in all that occurs; accept whatever happens as the will of God.

LOVE

We have spoken often about love. We have, in fact, presented an entire volume on the subject,* so complex and divine is it. But for now we will follow the approach of specifying various perspectives on love that are related to the overall theme of the book we are creating with you.

Love is the essence of the divine oversoul. It is an all-pervasive magnetic energy that is at once dominant and recessive. It is dominant in that no matter how strong and stealthy the forces of darkness, love will prevail in the end. We assure you of that. It is recessive in that the love-force pervades not so much because it defeats darkness with its mighty actions, but because it finds the smallest places to permeate and flows like water over boundaries and barriers alike, endlessly and effortlessly.

Love in all dimensions, including the third, is the life-force that stimulates creation. It is the primary element in all of matter and non-matter. If everything in the

---

*See *LoveLines* in the LifeLines Library

totality of the universes were to become nonexistent, there would still be one thing left, and it would be everywhere. That one thing is love.

Love finds its way into every situation. Its presence may be imperceptible to you, but it is there. Do not lose faith that love can and will infuse the circumstances of your daily life. It cannot not do so. For it is in everyone and everything—and cannot be extinguished.

Love in the higher dimensions might appear at first to be more powerful, for it is not mitigated by lower vibrational matter. As you traverse each dimension, the vibratory patterns that distinguish them develop a higher and higher frequency. These higher frequencies enable love to be present in a more pure form.

Nonetheless, love is fundamentally the same whether it exists in the third dimension or the eighteenth. For it is the God-force, and God remains unchanged—always, everywhere, forever.

You have as much access to love as we do. The difference is that the influence of its opposite is more apparent on the physical plane. Darkness may have an easier time occupying the lower-vibrational energy field of the third dimension, but it is equally viable on all planes. It shrouds itself differently based on the dimension in which it resides, and finds other ways to undermine the power of light-infused love.

Do not feel that your life on the earth plane is more loveless than it will be when you leave your physical body in death. The crystal of love embedded in all of life may be a bit harder for you to discover at the moment. But like the gold in the rock, it is there. It is also worth the effort of revealing it.

PATENT

You have a means on planet earth of protecting ideas and inventions, designs and discoveries, that an individual or a group develops. It is called a patent. Registering a patent for an idea establishes your legal ownership of it for a defined period of time and prevents others from copying or replicating it for their own gain. A similar standard is set with a copyright.

We do not take issue with patents and copyrights. They are necessary to help maintain order in a world distinguished by people without conscience who act from the premise that whatever they can appropriate without repercussions belongs to them. Protective measures are essential to keep squabbling and conflict to a minimum. Your worldwide business norms may be rooted in competition, but patents and copyrights of material and intellectual property help maintain relative integrity.

Did it ever occur to you, however, that you cannot own an idea and that, in fact, ideas that you believe you developed have never been yours in the first place? In the case of these channeled manuscripts, it is clear to you that the information and messages contained within them are not your singular creation. They are being dictated to you. You are a scribe, not an author. You do not feel that you own the material, although you have copyrighted it. That is reasonable.

But what if you understood that all of the ideas flying around the planet actually were derived from another source besides the person or team of people who dreamed them up? What if scientific discoveries occurred not so much because of controlled testing, but because the catalysts for their being uncovered were introduced into the magnetic intelligence surrounding the planet? What if new inventions occurred not because of huge investments in research and development, but because the embryos for them were seeded by higher consciousness into the earth's ether? What if you accepted the fact that there does exist an omniscient, omnipresent Creator, and that all discoveries derive from that source?

How would you feel about ownership then?

Pursue your patents; establish your copyrights; register your trademarks. But in doing so, be aware that the ideas and discoveries they are protecting do not really belong to you. You are merely acting as a steward for them—the guardian of a spark of knowledge that originated from spirit and eventually will return to the domain from whence it came.

OPENNESS

Your consideration of these messages, even if you do not entirely comprehend them, is evidence of your extraordinary openness to the ways of spirit. You would not be pursuing your study of these passages, some of which we acknowledge are almost unfathomable to you, if you did not have a high regard for what is available to you in the more distant realms.

You have opened your mind to learn about these realms. You have opened your consciousness to receive wisdom energetically. Both kinds of openness are essential if you are to imbibe the essence of these messages.

Openness springs forth from non-judging. Without faith you would close your mind to indications that an all-pervasive spiritual presence is integral to your every action, your every thought, your every breath. Without trust you would find rational reasons to discount the assertions made here, for they are not provable in your material world. And without non-judging, you would identify bases for the invalidation of every observation we make.

So the very fact that you are still reading these words rather than setting the book aside or tossing it away is ample proof of your intellectual openness to the concepts presented here. We encourage you to be intentional about this—to allow these ideas into your thought processes, even if they do not immediately make sense.

But your openness of consciousness is even more critical to your ability to integrate the power of these perspectives into your daily life. For your consciousness guides what you do in a subtle, almost imperceptible way. The more you imbibe the spiritual energy in these messages—the vibratory aspects that transcend the literal meaning of the content—the more capable you will be of aligning your thoughts, words and deeds with the spirit of these comments.

How do you remain open at the level of your higher consciousness? The best way to go about it is to unplug your left brain. Read a paragraph or a page, then close your eyes and cease to think about it. Instead experience the vibrations that are pulsing through your body as a result of your having imbibed these words. Let them become a part of your being as well as your brain. Allow them into your body consciousness, even if your intellect cannot exactly decipher them. Create a place within for them to reside, even if you are wont to define what is taking up residence.

Remain open to the consciousness as well as the composition, the clairvoyance as well as the content. They will serve you well.

OMNI

We have referred indirectly to the omnipresence, omniscience and omnipotence of the One. This ability to be everywhere at once, to know everything at once and to be all-powerful is the quality that distinguishes God from all of life. Even the most highly evolved spiritual masters in the highest etheric dimensions do not know as much as God. Even the most adept entities cannot be everywhere at once. Even the most potent angelic forces cannot exert power over all of creation.

God is omni. No one else and nothing else can be.

You are separate from God and yet the Creator lives within you. You feel the presence of spirit every time you are engulfed in a wave of optimism or when you act with uncompromising courage. You may not be omnipresent, but you certainly have the capability of being fully present with spirit wherever you are. You may not be all-knowing, but you can have faith that you will be given what you need to know as you continue to seek. You may not be able to harness the forces of nature, but you can flow with them as often as possible.

To try to be God-like in a way that intimates that you have power over others is to fall prey to hubris. To exert your control over others is to confuse power with potency. To tell others how to think or what to do is to presume that you know more than they do or that they are incapable of thinking for themselves. You cannot possibly know more about another than he himself does. How can you do his thinking for him?

God's abilities would, from the perspective of the material world, entitle this spirit to occupy the top of the grandest hierarchy that we might construct. God on earth would run the largest corporation, rule the most powerful government, be the richest billionaire in existence. Isn't that correct?

In considering this, think about the few times in the history of the planet when God manifested more fully as a human being in the form of a prophet. Did these prophets rule countries or stockpile armaments? Did they amass wealth or control hordes of people? Did they engage in grand displays of their omni qualities?

No, they did not. They were unpretentious servants of humanity, committed to embodying spirit with simple acts of kindness and compassion. They taught; they learned. They healed; they forgave. They suffered; they inspired.

God's presence within you has the potential of being as omni as it has been for the prophets. Your opportunity is to move toward your own omni-potential—humbly and with grace.

FOUNDATION

These messages are being communicated to help you build a stronger foundation for your ability to access the higher dimensions while you are still in this embodiment. On the one hand, you are living squarely in the material world and must keep the foundations for your life and livelihood there in good repair. On the other hand, you must become more capable of moving swiftly and decisively into the etheric planes. To do so requires a solid foundation on the other side.

What is this foundation composed of? How do you construct it? Where is it located? How will you know it is in place? These questions are appropriate, given how critical the foundation is to any structure you create in the third dimension. But in the higher dimensions, foundations take other forms.

The foundation for your ability to enter into higher and still higher realms is the degree to which you have integrated spirit into your life. Try as you might to build a foundation by repeating mantras or reciting affirmations, you will not integrate spirit more fully until your actions are grace-full. The more you exhibit generosity of heart and empathetic understanding toward others, the stronger your foundation will be in the spiritual realms.

Beyond that, what can you do to create a safe landing spot as you go higher and higher? First, unhook your ego from the desire to access the higher dimensions and then tell others about your capabilities. Your ego's job is to keep you from going there by making sure that you remain firmly rooted in third-dimensional priorities.

Next, clarify that your motivations are pure and your intention is to do the work of spirit more effectively. Do not look for milestones; refrain from judging your progress; allow yourself to be flexibly in-the-moment instead of invested in a particular result. See the reality beyond your immediate reality. Make it as much a part of you as your home and your circle of family and friends are.

You see, then, that this foundation for accessing the higher realms is really a non-foundation from a third-dimensional perspective. The very act of trying to create a permanent one makes it elusive. It is ever emerging, always flowing, perpetually impermanent. You will find that the more you move beyond the physical world, the more freely you will establish your foundation on the other side. Like a magnet you will fly toward it, carrying your higher consciousness along with you and leaving your physical body like baggage behind.

Continue to prepare for your ever more frequent and profound excursions to the other realities. They nurture your spirit and reaffirm your soul. Know that every time you go there you are strengthening your foundation for that aspect of your existence. Be grateful for the opportunity to do so.

FORWARD

You want nothing more than to know that you are moving forward on your pilgrimage to spirit. Your belief is that progress is measured by your ability to trust in the wisdom of your inner voice. You think that you are moving forward when you hear it clearly and act upon it unerringly. You assume that your progress has been halted when you hear nothing and feel as if you are wandering in the wilderness.

How can you tell if you are going forward, backward or sideways? Where do you look for feedback? What do you use to measure how far you have gone?

In the higher dimensions, where time and space have ceased to be factors of consequence, there is no way to differentiate forward and backward movement. All things exist everywhere and can be everywhere at all times. So advancement as you know it is not a measurable phenomenon. Forward movement and backward movement both lead to the same place. Inside and outside merge rather than mirroring each other. To progress you must sometimes regress.

You carry the burden of your third-dimensional orientation toward an efficiency-based definition of success. You value the direct route over the convoluted one. You detest detours and object to obstacles. You would rather drive in fifth gear in the fast lane than wander in the wilderness. Forward is your preferred modus operandi; reverse is annoying, to say the least.

We invite you to reconsider these postulations, for they are withholding from you a great deal of valuable insight and experience. What causes you to want to go forward all the time? Most likely it is impatience mixed with a hefty dose of uncertainty. You try to alleviate your impatience and assuage your uncertainty by blasting ahead on something—anything—in order to create the illusion of having made progress. You are proficient at this, as are many people on the planet these days.

We are sending down these messages so that you will be able to approach the higher realms with greater clarity of purpose and certainty of commitment. No doubt they will lead some of you to take great strides forward—to make far more progress than you ever imagined possible. But we caution you not to get so caught up in your spiritual renaissance that you decide the only way to achieve it is to go charging forward. If you do that, you will jeopardize the quintessential quality of the experience—that backward can be forward and standing still can be the catalyst for the greatest progress of all.

Embrace the opportunities we are offering you, but do so with a light heart free of striving and solemnity. Yes, this is serious business, but it is also a joyful occasion. When your heart is overflowing with love, you will know that you have gone forward toward spirit.

COMMON SENSE

Something is common sense to you when it is rooted in third-dimensional assumptions. For instance, it is common sense not to squander your money. It is common sense to wear warm clothing in the winter. It is common sense to plan ahead for a big event or to talk honestly with your physician about your health.

Indeed, all of that makes sense. Common sense.

Along a wide swath of your life you do what is sensible because, for the most part, it works for you. Being sensible is a good thing, isn't it?

Yes it is, up to a point. But if you allow common sense to guide too much of your life, you will create unnecessary limitations in many areas of your existence. Is it common sense to believe that you might be able to access the higher dimensions, and therefore you should invest precious time in contemplating this possibility? No, not really. Is it common sense to see your immediate reality in terms of how it might appear through the lens of timelessness and spacelessness? No, not at all.

Common sense is a phenomenon of the material world.

In the higher realms nothing is common, and very little is sensible as you picture it. In the higher realms everything is unique, and much of it is inconceivable to you.

It is not necessary to use common sense on the etheric plane because spirit is so much more present there. Guidance from high teachers is far more apparent than it is on the earth plane. Those beings help inform choices with a rich reality that mirrors the complexities of their more evolved spiritual essence. From that perspective, common sense would hold you back.

When you traverse the higher dimensions, you realize that much of what is quite real to you there makes no sense on the earthly plane. You might be aware of a strong possibility that a major change will occur. You might even be able to see it as clearly as you would if it were actually occurring. But from the perspective of the third dimension, that possibility is unfathomable. There is no way you could justify believing it could occur. Why? Because it defies common sense.

Before you discount out of hand what others might be seeing or feeling or thinking because it does not make sense, ask yourself this:

♦ According to what criteria is this not sensible?
♦ What might I not be able to see right now that would set the stage for this potentiality?
♦ Am I so wedded to the physical plane that I will not consider that there might be other circumstances in which soul and spirit could exist?
♦ What am I avoiding? What am I missing? What am I hiding from?

It only makes sense to do that, doesn't it?

TRIAL and ERROR

You have a feedback mechanism called trial and error that stimulates efficient learning and provides an ongoing source of information. You take a step, see what happens as a result, adjust what you are doing, take another step, see what happens, and so on. The process of trial and error enables you to limit your exposure to big risks and obtain valuable input much more quickly than you would otherwise.

Even in the higher dimensions trial and error is worthwhile. We often cannot predict exactly what will happen, so we use all of our available wisdom and knowledge to make the best possible choice, then monitor the impact of our decisions.

The distinction we want to make here is one of degrees—not of right and wrong. The process of trial and error that we follow in the higher dimensions has a different definition of error because we are following a different purpose for our trials.

What we are trying out is our ability to create new frames and forms of thinking, which then manifest as action. We visualize an alternative then watch how it plays out over the long term. All of this happens in what, from a third-dimensional perspective, would be a millisecond. If we need to make corrections, we do so in our next visualization. In the blink of an eye we can test a dozen scenarios and determine their potential impact.

How is that possible? If everything past, present and future exists all at once, then it would not be difficult for us to experience the potentiality, probability and inevitability of something simultaneously. What you might see only as a possibility from a material perspective could look more probable to us. What may appear to be an inevitability from your vantage point might be a non-event from our perspective.

Consider how you use the process of trial and error.

♦ What are you attempting to discover when you are trying something out? Is it narrow in scope or more expansive? Is it prescribed or open-ended? Does it assume predictability or unpredictability?

♦ How will you be attending to the feedback you get? Will you be perceiving it from the position of what you can quantify and measure? Will you be using rational, linear ways to understand what is going on, or will your intuition come into play as well? Are you keeping your predispositions out of the way so that you can be truly unbiased regarding the input you are getting?

♦ How are you interpreting error? Is error something that does not conform to the outcome you anticipate? Are you anticipating any particular outcome at all? How willing would you be to acknowledge the outliers—the data that make no sense at all from a material perspective? Would you force-fit them into the frame you are comfortable with, or would you remain open to the new plausibility they represent?

The more you can release your circumscribed presumptions about how the world works (which do not in the slightest represent how it actually works) and allow truly fresh impressions to emerge, the more effective your trial-and-error processes will be.

QUANTUM

The word *quantum* refers to the discontinuous emission or absorption of energy, with an emphasis on the word *discontinuous*. Everything in creation has the potential of making a quantum shift from one state of existence or consciousness to another. There are no inherent limits to what you can do or be or become. You may experience self-imposed limits, but they can be discarded just as easily as they are adopted.

Quantum changes in your evolutionary trajectory occur as a result of incremental, perhaps even imperceptible, steps that you take over an extended period of time. You may experience nothing different for quite a while; you may even lose heart, believing that no matter how hard you try or what you do, it will never be enough. Then suddenly, with no warning and very little effort, you reach a new level of development. You experience yourself differently. The only thing that links the current "you" with the former "you" is the one additional step you took or choice you made. On the surface it appeared to be similar to all of the others, and in some ways it was.

Except that it wasn't.

You have just experienced a quantum leap. Quantum leaps occur when advances in quality and increases in quantity merge to form a new actuality. Here is how it works: Perhaps you want to be able to meditate so deeply that you can experience total peace. You take meditation classes, read books on meditation techniques, and practice meditation regularly. But each time you sit, you cannot seem to clear your mind of the mundane aspects of life. Your brain's constant chatter distracts you. The peace you desire seems elusive, if not impossible.

Then one day, just like any other, you sit in meditation. In a flash (albeit a quiet one) you find yourself in the void. It is an empty pool of nothingness. You realize what has just happened and think, "I did it!" at which point the void vanishes and your brain is chattering away again. But for a moment you were there.

You just took a quantum leap.

Over time you will enter into the void more easily and stay there longer. You may even be able to experience almost unlimited suspensions of earthly reality. But none of those advancements will represent as quantum a leap as you took the moment you encountered the void for the first time. That occurrence was discontinuous; the subsequent ones are continuous along the new path onto which you launched yourself.

Remember this the next time you become impatient because you do not believe you are making any headway. Your efforts to integrate spirit more completely into your life require discipline and fortitude and constant attention. They also require faith that even when you feel as if you are regressing, if your intention is to honor the spirit inherent in all things, you are progressing. You never know when the quantity and quality of your actions will reach the quantum point—and you will discover yourself in a totally altered state of being.

CALIBRATE

You calibrate much of what occurs in your life. That is neither incorrect nor inappropriate. The question is this: Are your calibrations originating from a place of discernment or disregard, mindfulness or myopia?

You can fine-tune the details of your life from either province. If you remain conscious of the larger impact of your choices, your calibrations will lead you to higher-order understanding. If you are unconscious, your calibrations will keep you entrenched in material reality.

Contemplate for a moment what you would calibrate if time and space parameters did not exist. Start by creating a representative list of what you would not calibrate. You would calibrate nothing related to when or where, for there would be no when or where to calibrate. That leaves you with who, what, how and why.

- The *who* you would calibrate would be your enlightened self.
- The *what* you would calibrate would be your energy.
- The *how* you would calibrate would be your attention and intention.

- The *why* you would calibrate would be your higher purpose.

Reality in the higher realms is composed of the vibration of spirit. Your existence in the higher realms is composed of your enlightened self as you expend energy with the intention of achieving a higher purpose. That is what you calibrate.

Now consider what you calibrate on the physical plane. Most of your attention is focused on regulating the timing of something or the space-based consequences of your actions, whether they take the form of income or information, travel or trade. The who, what, how and why look something like this:

- The *who* you calibrate is your presentation of self in the external world.
- The *what* you calibrate is your level of investment and risk.
- The *how* you calibrate is your intellect complemented by your intuition.
- The *why* you calibrate is your desire to gain more than you lose.

What if you were to substitute the calibrations you make in the higher dimensions for the ones you construct on the earthly plane?

Is it possible? Indeed, it is.

Is it reasonable? Why wouldn't it be?

Is it worthwhile? Only if you hunger to transcend the limits of time and space while you inhabit that selfsame time and space on earth.

ALCHEMY

Alchemy involves the transmutation of a base metal into a precious metal. The Egyptians had that capability, having derived it from Atlanteans who brought it with them before the island sank into the ocean. A few medieval Merlins were alchemists, although many more claimed they had succeeded in it than those who actually did.

You might believe that the stories of alchemists are merely legends, embellished by troubadours to make their myths more fantastic. Alchemy lends itself to legend. For those living a materialistic world, what would be better than to have the capability of creating something so rare and valuable from something so ordinary and worthless? Indeed, to be able to turn lead into gold would spark the imagination immensely.

But alchemy is possible. It is not a branch of the tree of mythology. Planet earth has seen a number of adept alchemists over the millennia. Where did they come from? How did they learn to transmute metals and other substances?

Alchemy is no more complicated, really, than many of the more mundane procedures that create chemical compounds. It does, however, require a capability that few possess. For to be an alchemist, one must infuse the base metal with such an intense and incessant vibratory charge that its molecular composition shifts. On the one hand, you can break down metal and gold into their individual chemical components. On the other hand, the only way you can transform the former into the latter is to change the magnetics of the mass. And the way you change those magnetics is to bring down spirit.

The Atlanteans understood the power of spirit. They used it on a daily basis to heal, to manufacture, to maintain the community, to prevent aging. The temples in Atlantis were established as power spots designated for the express purpose of maintaining a strong degree of love and blanketing the community with it. But access to spirit was integral to everyday life as well. What you perceive as bizarre or impossible was mundane to them. They were keenly aware every moment of every day that they were as much spirit as flesh, if not more so. And they lived their lives accordingly, until Atlantis began its precipitous fall.

Their base metals were no different in composition from what you have today. Their gold was no different. What differed was their understanding of the union of spirit with every aspect of the material world. They experienced spirit vibrating in the rocks as much as in their priests engaged in ecstatic meditation. You tend not to see the spirit in inanimate objects, as you call them. But they are just as animate as you are—and just as capable of vibrating at an extremely high frequency.

Alchemy, then, occurs when constricted assumptions about the pervasive existence of spirit are replaced with an unfailing belief that spirit dwells in everything. At that point a spiritual adept is capable of infusing a mass of molecules with penetrating vibrations that, indeed, can turn inert lead into glistening gold.

ALCHEMY
REVISITED

There is another way to consider the implications of the alchemical process. From a spiritual perspective the "base metal" is the unevolved individual existing entirely on the material plane, and the "precious metal" consists of his or her enlightenment. Alchemy, then, is the transformation of mortal flesh into immortal spirit.

Death is not synonymous with alchemy, for in death the soul is released from the confines of the body and is once again given the wings to fly free. Liberation is not transformation. To liberate is to unfetter—to leave the original state behind. To transform is to metamorphose—to change into something wholly unlike the original.

Alchemy requires faith, for without faith it is impossible to align yourself with spirit. And alchemy demands exquisite alignment with spirit.

Alchemy also requires trust, for without trust you would never choose to traverse the oblivion that lies between one state of being and another.

Finally, alchemy requires resolve, for without resolve you would turn back at the first sign of uncertainty.

This book is about spiritual alchemy—the transcendence of your way of being during this lifetime from existence to essence.

Existence to essence. What does that mean?

You life on earth revolves around the purpose of surviving for as long as you can while you achieve the highest possible quality of life. A long life lived well is optimal. A long life is measured in terms of years; a life lived well is measured in terms of physical health, creature comforts, intellectual agility, aesthetic enhancements, supportive relationships and material security. Those are the parameters of your existence.

But your life on earth is also blessed with essence. You are spirit in the flesh. You are born with that quality, and it will remain with you until this embodiment is complete. In some ways you may think that alchemy is unnecessary because you already are spirit.

Alchemy occurs when you live your life more from a base of spirit than of flesh—when the thoughts you think and the choices you make are rooted in your comprehension of the impact they will have on all of creation rather than on your immediate well-being. Alchemy explodes your previous fears, judgments and conflicts, turning them into fairy dust. Alchemy creates a love within you that is so fathomless, so inviolable, that no matter what the circumstances of your existence, you are first and foremost essence.

Alchemy is the most incomparable gift that the Creator has bestowed upon all of conscious nature. It is the gift of love; it is the promise of enlightenment as well as eternal life. It is what makes your existence worth the struggle and the attainment of your essence worth the loss of your former self. It is what brings you closer to God, and what brings God more fully within you.

UNFOLDING

You close your eyes and see a path before you. It represents your future, as you call the months and years you have not yet experienced on the material plane. The path extends so far into the future, you cannot see the end of it. Along the way, your life in your current human embodiment will unfold.

On the higher planes this unfolding has no linear time frame, as it does in the earthly dimension. What you label past, present and future are concurrent. Simultaneously you have reached the culmination of your journey—you are at the end of the path—and you are still in the process of experiencing it.

When you begin to access the higher dimensions more frequently and completely, you will start to experience a number of unusual phenomena.

First, you will lose a portion of your grounding in time and space. Without a precise calendar of reminders, you will forget appointments you have made. Without a map or directions you will become lost, even if you are going to familiar places. Time will speed up, slow down, stop—all in a disconcertingly discontinuous way. Distances will stretch and contract; places will change polarities. Many of the ways that you used to routinize your life will come unglued.

Next, you will discover that the fears that used to bedevil you and the desires that used to motivate you no longer have the influence they once had. You do not react the same way you might have before. You watch yourself being someone you never used to be. You are at once intrigued and intimidated. Who is this person? How do I know if she is just visiting or taking up permanent residence?

Then there are your relationships, which become both more profound and more problematic. Those with people who are on the path with you become more fundamental and fulfilling. Those with people who are not progressing with you become strained and superficial. You have little patience for the latter. You have all the patience in the world for the former, for therein lies your destiny and destination.

And finally, you notice that a calm comes over you unbidden, reaffirming that things are unfolding exactly as they should. You haven't any idea of where you are headed with your life, but it doesn't matter anymore. You no longer need a predictable plan; you relish the excursion as much as its conclusion. In truth you cannot conceive of a conclusion. You see instead journey after journey, path after path—all of them leading to God. You know that you will have arrived nowhere until you are at one with the One.

This brings you peace of mind. Your life is unfolding as it should. You are at once familiar with who you are and just becoming acquainted with who you are becoming. There are interludes of joy amidst the determination, and absolute knowing amidst the vague inklings.

You are on your way. You have also already arrived.

COMMERCE

Commerce is the business of bartering or exchanging a product or service of value for another of equal value as determined by the parties involved. For millennia communities have ripened and decayed based on the commerce associated with them. Individuals spend much of the time and energy that is available to them occupied with commerce. It is the lifeblood of many earthly cultures.

Consider the commerce in which you are currently engaged. You can easily track from a material perspective what you expend for what you gain, what you invest and what you receive in return. You have a relatively clear idea of the value you are willing to offer in exchange for the benefits you derive. Most of your agreements are up-front and above-board. That is best in the commercial arena.

Does commerce occur in spiritual domains? Do exchanges occur anywhere besides on earth? You may be surprised to learn that your planet does not have a lock on commercialism. It may be called something else in other places, and the ends may be more focused on spiritual advancement than on wealth accumulation, but everywhere living beings are engaged in trading one aspect of themselves for something in return.

What form does this trade take? What could be traded if there were no material things—if there were no time clocks, no workplaces, no banks, no shopping malls? The answer is as direct as it is circuitous. What you exchange is potentiality for actuality and prognostication for culmination. The opposite is true as well. You exchange actuality for potentiality and culmination for prognostication.

Let us explain. In the higher realms your assets consist of your capacity to grow spiritually. That is the greatest asset any being could possess. It is also not something that anyone can own. It is a gift from God—the one gift that is given to you and never taken away. It is inherent in all of creation; it is also inherent in all that you are. You can either act from the base of that potential or squander it.

You make that choice in the higher dimensions with everything you do. You can be love, in which case you exchange nothing at all. Your love multiplies many-fold rather than being spent or traded for something else. Or you can be less than loving, in which case you exchange all of your potential to grow in spirit for either stagnation or regression.

The same is true for the commerce in which you are engaged on the physical plane. What are you exchanging, really, and what are you getting in return for it, really? Your answers may surprise you. What appears to be an easily calculable transaction may be exacting from you an incalculable toll. You may be bargaining your soul for your financial security. You may be sacrificing your peace of mind to maximize profitability.

Commerce on the material plane doesn't necessarily come at a cost to spirit. But it does often enough that it is worth your while to do some soul-searching in that regard.

RENAISSANCE

Your ability to transcend the limits of the material world and approach the higher realms will spark nothing short of a renaissance in your life. Your former attitudes and assumptions will lose their power over your thought patterns. Their credibility in your daily life will diminish. You will replace structure with sensing and prescription with perception. Your understanding of your life's work will dawn with greater clarity than you ever thought possible. Your existence will become more serene; former attachments will fall away, leaving you with fewer complications and encumbrances.

This reawakening of consciousness will occur in the context of a world still slumbering under the influence of materialism. Your task is not to convince others of the restrictions inherent in their worldview, nor is it to save them from themselves (from your vantage point, at least). Rather, it is to continue on your own course unfailingly and remain open to meeting up with other pilgrims along the way.

The rebirth of your being into higher consciousness

will enable you to experience as a reality what others believe is nonexistent. It will disable your dependence on worldly acquisitions and wealth for a sense of security. It will disarm your fears and sweep away your judgments. You will spend more time alone and be acutely aware of occasions when you are being less than yourself for whatever reason. The more mindful people around you will notice a difference in you; the less aware will be either oblivious to the changes in you or will determine that they are a result of a failing on your part.

As with any significant transformation, you will be swimming against the tide of consistency and conformity. You must not resist it. You must not participate in it or partake of it. Instead, recognize that your consistency will be more aligned with spirit than with the material world. Your conformity will manifest as attunement with God rather than uniformity with mass culture.

You may look like everyone else and wear the same jeans as everyone else and live in the same neighborhood as everyone else, but you are not like everyone else. You must neither prove that you are not like others nor prove that you are exactly like others. Either objective is irrelevant.

Your purpose is to see love and light everywhere and to be love and light in everything you do. It is to release the need to acquire anything other than the wisdom that derives from conscious knowing. It is to sidestep the seductions whispered by priorities aimed at eroding your sense of self and your ability to see God in all that is.

The renaissance you are experiencing is an inner one. Its outer manifestations are not high art and architecture, but higher consciousness and humble mindfulness. Many others are encountering it along with you. You will recognize each other. They are the people in your neighborhood and in other communities around the world wearing jeans and making a living just like you. But they are also making a life of love and light, just like you.

Welcome them. Acknowledge their own renaissance. For like yours, it is holy.

TRAVEL

You travel through time and space using various means and media. Some of them are recognizable to you; others appear to be quite foreign, even though you use them all the time.

You are familiar with the vehicles that transport you from one location to another in the third dimension. You can walk or pedal a bicycle. You can ride in a bus or subway, drive a car or truck, fly in an airplane. All of these mechanisms have one purpose: to enable you to move your physical body. Such movement is an inherent part of life on the planet. Without it you would be significantly less effective than you are.

But there are other means of travel that you employ more often than you know. They do not require advance reservations or ticket purchases. You do not have to board them or fill them with gasoline or change the oil. This is possible because they are magnetic in nature. These vibratory vehicles transport your energy-body instantaneously.

You ride in a carriage called the soul. It transports

you from one lifetime to the next and in between them—century after century, millennium after millennium. Your soul is your spaceship as well, traveling between spiritual realms whether you are in embodiment or existing completely in the higher dimensions.

There has never been a more practical yet superbly built carriage than the one your soul provides you. It has more memory than the capacity of the largest supercomputer ever built. It can move instantaneously from one plane of existence to another. It can combine with others to form an intergalactic caravan without creating gridlock.

Your soul is a fine carriage, indeed.

You spend most of your life oblivious to the places your soul is taking you in its travels, the conversations you have with spirits when you get there, and the adventures you experience along the way. Everything you think, say and do in your life has an impact on your soul. And in turn, your soul can carry you far beyond whatever you think, say and do—if you give it the opportunity to contribute to your life in that way.

Refrain from discounting insights that seem to make no sense to you. Do not be stymied by discontinuities that defy rationality. They may represent a swatch of the cosmic tapestry that your soul acquired as it was traveling beyond time and space.

Open your consciousness to the faraway places you can go in your soul-travel. Remember your dreams; attend to your intuitive flashes; look beyond the obvious for the meaning behind the apparent meaning. That will enable you to discover more about where your soul is taking you, and what is revealed to you while you are there.

JOY

The more adept you become at accessing the higher dimensions, the more joyful your life will become as well. But that joy will be qualitatively different from what you typically consider to be a joyous state. The feeling will be so unique, in fact, that you might not recognize it as joy.

Joy as you know it is a peak experience of gladness— an exalted state of bliss. You remember times in your life when you have been joyful, so intense was the feeling. Do not generalize from those experiences to the ones you are likely to have as you begin to access the etheric realities. If you do that, you will be looking for the wrong sensation.

You associate joy with ecstasy. You are accustomed to thinking of it as being more like a tsunami than a bubbling brook. It does manifest in that way, but much of the drama associated with joy is an artifact of the lack of joy in the third dimension. In other words, the contrast between joy and the joyless steady state that pervades the material world is so absolute, it takes on much greater significance than it would otherwise have.

When you leave this plane and enter into the higher realms, that contrast becomes almost nonexistent. Joy is fundamental to the life of spirit. Wherever spirit dwells, there is joy. So when you take your consciousness to the inner planes, where spirit is the dominant force, joy is inherent in everything you do and feel. Joy in a more highly evolved state is a constant—something so thoroughly united with your being that you become accustomed to it. It is rather like your heartbeat—subtle but always there.

This joy manifests as a quiet inner knowing that all that is, is perfect in its current state of being. This perfection exists because God is in all that is, and God is perfect. You sense that all is right with the world even if, from an external perspective, it is difficult to identify much at all that is right with the world.

You have the capability to experience joy every moment of every day, no matter what is occurring all around you. That joy will be your salvation amidst the chaos into which humanity sometimes throws itself. It will be your navigational instrument as you find your way through the fears and manipulations that obstruct the material world. It will provide you with comfort when there is nowhere else to turn for it.

Joy is the heartbeat of spirit, the delicate vibration that whispers and affirms the presence of spirit. It both inspires and is inspired by your faith. It is all that you need and only a small fraction of what you can attain. It enables you to savor the divine everywhere you go, knowing that you are never without love.

LINEAGE

The lineage that many of you are following is from a soul group committed to bringing light and love into all of God's universes. One locale where this group has been focusing much energy and attention—and where many members have taken embodiment again and again—is planet earth. We see great opportunity on the planet; we also see great resistance to the changes that are likely to occur within the next two or three decades.

Understand that this lineage is committed to its mission and will do everything possible to enable its achievement. We use nonviolent means to counteract the forces of darkness. We bring light in all of its manifestations— philosophy, music, art, love, beauty, nature. We shed the light of insight in the darkest recesses of the mind; we help create families and governments with underpinnings of love, trust and respect. We catalyze grand social experiments, many of which have shaped the global community.

We will not cease our endeavors on earth and elsewhere until the totality of creation is at one with God. Throughout infinity, as we have been working toward this goal, we have seen more failures than successes. Nonetheless, the successes far outweigh the failures because of their qualitative influence over the spiritual ecology of the species in question. We have been born into places almost devoid of light. Over and over again we took form there, with little progress to show for our efforts. Finally a crack in the armor of darkness appeared, and that crack became a fissure, then a chasm, and eventually darkness was torn asunder.

We are far from obliterating darkness on planet earth. But we are pleased, nonetheless, with the progress being made. Our lineage requires that we see the light in all that is—that we love without bonds and forgive without hesitation. This challenges each soul in the lineage to pursue individual spiritual development vigorously. For nothing less than total dedication to the light and openness of heart will suffice.

Embrace the opportunity to contribute to this worthy mission. Prepare yourself to be light wherever you are and whatever the occasion. You cannot fathom the degree to which your light strengthens and heals yourself and others. You cannot recognize the value of your commitment to the light. You cannot associate yourself with a more meritorious cause than that of spreading light throughout God's creation.

It starts, of course, with your own immediate sphere: your home, your work, your family and friends, your community, your written laws and unwritten cultural codes. All of these have far-reaching influence. They also comprise varying degrees of darkness and light. Wherever there is darkness, there is work to be done. Wherever there is light, there is nourishment to share.

You honor or dishonor this lineage with your mental attitudes, communication and conduct. The lineage will remain throughout eternity. It is your choice how you integrate the enlightenment of its heritage.

SHIFT

These messages link aeons of spiritual progress with the corresponding context activated on planet earth at the end of the second millennium A.D. Your current degree of spiritual development is both inadequate to stimulate an evolutionary leap and more than what you need to fuel such a shift.

It is inadequate in that the masses of humanity have not yet achieved access to the higher dimensions—and the wisdom that is available within them. So they will be unable to guide the evolution in an incremental way toward oneness with spirit.

It is more than enough because a critical mass of souls in embodiment on the planet at this time have found the gateway to the higher dimensions and are accessing the enlightenment available there. They will put it to good use in the transformation of the planet. But because the transformation will occur as a result of a critical mass and not a majority, it is more likely to take the form of revolutionary change than incremental change.

Whether this change occurs as a result of successive

smaller steps forward or one big leap is irrelevant. The key is that you are moving in the right direction—and quite quickly, as a matter of fact. Every day more and more of you are integrating spiritual discipline into the warp and woof of your lives. Every day more of you choose light and love than ever before.

We are grateful for that.

Do not concern yourself with the timing of the shift or with what its catalyst will be. We cannot predict any of this, nor can you. You cannot plan it; you cannot force people to support it; you cannot cajole others into doing something before they are ready or accomplishing something they do not have the capability to achieve.

But what you can do is find your own edge—that place where you are challenging yourself to the core of your spiritual being—and go right up to it. Do that again and again and again. Create your boundaries; clarify your priorities; bring all that you are into each moment of your life.

Every transformation starts from within; every revolution begins with a thought; every incremental step toward change occurs because someone chose to take a first step in a different direction.

Your responsibilities are considerable, but they also start and end with yourself. Focusing on what everyone else must do to make something happen enables you to sidestep your own accountabilities. Refrain from being beguiled by such considerations, for they will tempt you away from your real work. And that work is with yourself.

If you long for world peace; if your heart breaks every time you hear of another human or ecological tragedy; if you have lost respect for those who hold the power; if the problems all seem so huge that they are certain to be a lost cause, stop right there. Ask yourself what you can do right at this moment to share or affirm the love in your life. Then do it.

ABANDON

Used as a verb, to abandon someone or something is to relinquish it, to leave it behind. Used as a noun, to do something with abandon is to approach it without barriers—to do so spontaneously and enthusiastically.

We are not asking you to abandon your life on the material plane in order to integrate the higher realms more fully into your life. Such drastic action is not necessary. Nor must you be abandoned by others because you have begun to experience heretofore unavailable spiritual aspects in your life. If you are at ease with your new discoveries, you need not alienate anyone so significantly that they want you out of their lives.

But you must abandon your predispositions to see whatever occurs solely from the lens of the third dimension. When you see like that, you are unnecessarily limiting what you can access and perceive. Yes, the third dimension is one legitimate aspect of your reality and yes, it does provide valuable information. But it is not the only reality in which you reside and thus does not deserve to occupy a central role in your thinking.

When you become more deeply united with the etheric realms, they begin to influence how you perceive everything going on around you. Rather than attending to the myriad details and detours that used to take you from your path, you find that you become heedless of them. Things that used to aggravate you become inconsequential. People who before frustrated you or made you angry or fearful lose their ability to hook you into their viewpoints.

Instead you notice what they are doing and feel quite detached from it. You see clearly what is happening, and you understand why it is occurring. You recognize that it is someone else's life choice—not your own.

When you notice yourself doing that, you have abandoned your need to gain your legitimacy from earthly dynamics and the people who participate in them.

Coupled with that comes an unfamiliar sense of abandon. You find that you "just know" what you need to do, and you commit to it with a minimum of hand-wringing or hesitation. You replace calculation with trust and convolution with directness. Your approach is, This is what I will do and how I will do it. You are open to feedback, but you are also totally objective about it. If others' viewpoints enhance your thinking, you consider them. If they constrain your thinking, you set them aside.

Such a high degree of abandon may seem reckless to others, who interpret your words and actions as being unsubstantiated and risky. From your perspective, however, they are as solid as anything could be. But then, your perspective has at its core a number of intangibles, some of which you are aware of and some of which you are not.

Do not doubt the abandon with which you become accustomed to living your life. It represents the core of your being—not the periphery. It is more real than what others might label reality. It is as elusive to them as it is accessible to you.

ANCESTORS

You are not quite the trailblazer you believe yourself to be. At times you may feel that you are traversing uncharted terrain. But you are not. The way has been paved for you by many who have gone before you. The way has also been paved by you during prior lifetimes, when you acted on your convictions despite the tide of opposition.

Your spiritual ancestors have been arriving on planet earth from the higher realms for millennia, taking embodiment to help advance the enlightened evolution of the species. Sometimes they were in positions of political or religious power; sometimes they led humble lives, giving unconditionally to family and community. However their lifetimes were configured, they left the planet a better place than it was when they landed here.

Much of their work involved setting the stage for what is transpiring now. Often they were less concerned with overt, measurable progress than they were with leading inherently integrity-filled lives. Sometimes, however, they engineered breakthroughs of magnificent proportions. Leonardo da Vinci and Michelangelo were spiritual ancestors, as were Joan of Arc and Hildegard von Bingen. Most of the American founding fathers were from one spiritual group, having agreed to be born at the same time and to make their way to the new continent so that they could create a truly inspired set of parameters for living together. Ralph Waldo Emerson was a spiritual forefather, as were Albert Einstein, Mahatma Gandhi and Martin Luther King. The Dalai Lama is. So is Jimmy Carter.

Why are we telling you this? What does it matter? We hope that it will reassure you to know that you are not alone—that you are an extension of a long and continuing tradition of wisdom and righteousness. All of your spiritual ancestors, whether they led modest or magnificent lives, have made the path a bit less hazardous for you—and a bit more fruitful. You are able to sidestep invisible barriers and keep to your course more precisely because of their groundwork.

What was that groundwork? How does it affect you now?

Remember that in the higher dimensions time and space do not exist. Leonardo da Vinci saw far ahead of his time and space constraints, creating inventions that defied the accepted reality of the Italian Renaissance. By envisioning and drawing his inventions, da Vinci fueled their manifestation during later centuries and constructed the reality before it was actualized in the third dimension.

Everything your spiritual ancestors have envisioned —and it is a love-based planet, indeed—has already been achieved, even though you may not see overt evidence of it yet. Every step they took helps make your steps steadier and firmer. Every word they wrote or uttered has been catalogued in the archives of spirit—and in the collective consciousness of all of humanity. You are at one with them and what they sought to accomplish. You are not alone. Quite the contrary, you are in exceptional company.

BEING

The evolution of your soul throughout and between lifetimes involves a fluid interplay of being and non-being. Being focuses on your actions and accomplishments, decisions and declarations. Non-being occurs when you release all of that and become integrated with the elixir of spirit.

Your being is your soul. Your non-being is your soul. When your soul leaves your body upon death, being and non-being merge within it, pulsating in unison with the magnetics of the etheric realms.

When your soul takes embodiment, it sacrifices that unity. Part of it begins to dwell within and immediately around your physical body, playing an active role in your being-ness. It is the center for spirit within you. This aspect of your soul helps guide your actions, encouraging you to make more love-based choices. It helps you remain aware that you are spirit as well as flesh, despite the obvious third-dimensional reality that surrounds you. Although most of this aspect of your soul is involved with being, it also subtly fosters your non-being.

Another equally vital portion of your soul continues to explore and engage in the higher realms even after you have taken birth. This part of your soul embodies both being and non-being. On the one hand, it enables you to participate in actions and activities occurring in the higher dimensions. That is being. On the other hand, it simply is. It exists in a state of near oneness with God. It joins with pure essence. It vibrates in unison with all that is.

You are far more than what you perceive. You derive from the fountainhead of creation. Yes, you are a soul in a body at the time of the second millennium A.D. on planet earth. That soul in that body has thoughts and feelings, personality and character, aesthetic tastes and creative outlets, intelligence and intuition. You are all of that. You are also your memories and anticipations, your gratitude and regrets.

Beyond that, you are boundless spirit. You are a multifaceted soul with the ability to approach the realms of higher consciousness with grace and wisdom. You are moments of silence, when all that you hear is your breathing and your heartbeat and all that you know is that you are at peace. You are more than you ever dreamed you could be.

You are more than enough.

Recognize how your being and non-being dance together throughout the day. Become more aware of the contribution each can make in turn to the life that is immediately before you and the one that you live beyond the veil. Welcome their pulsating rhythms. For theirs is the dance of creation manifest within you, who are a most magnificent presence in the eternal choreography.

VOID

Beyond timelessness and spacelessness is another reality. It is the void. This void is nothingness. It contains nonexistence, and yet it encompasses all of creation. It is where pure spirit originated and continues to dwell in its most complete and unadulterated form. It is the place of non-movement, non-involvement and non-judging. It is all and nothing, void and completeness. It is finality and potentiality, path and wilderness.

It is the stillness that meditators seek. It is the place of longing and fulfillment. It is a home for the soul that sustains nothing except nothingness.

It is the reality beyond the higher realities; the dimension that transcends every dimension; the joy that derives from non-feeling; the fulfillment that emanates from total surrender; the wisdom inherent in knowing that knowing is unnecessary.

It is the whole embodied in the void.

Gates McKibbin never imagined that after spending twenty years as a corporate executive, management consultant and adjunct college professor specializing in strategic and organizational renewal, she would publish messages channeled from her deceased father, John McKibbin. For most of her adult life she had balanced a fulfilling professional career and a fascinating spiritual quest. Then quite unexpectedly her father, who visited the earth plane frequently after his death, began sending telepathic messages for her to write in her journal.

Three years and six books later, Gates has now added "Inspirational author and speaker" to her resume. She still helps business executives navigate turbulent change, and she also seeds the planet with insights from the spirit world. To complement the LifeLines Library, Gates has developed a collection of thematic LifeLines note pads featuring her favorite one-liners from the books.

Born and raised in central Illinois, Gates now resides in San Francisco. Whenever she has a few hours of free time, she hunts for vintage jackets, walks to North Beach restaurants for risotto, creates bead-bedecked greeting cards and, of course, continues her journal writing. Gates holds a Ph.D. from the University of Illinois and has received numerous academic awards, among them Phi Beta Kappa.

LIFELINES LIBRARY ORDER FORM

Book Title	Quantity	Total Cost
The Light in the Living Room: Dad's Messages from the Other Side **$9.95**		
LoveLines: Notes on Loving and Being Loved **$9.95**		
A Course in Courage: Disarming the Darkness with Strength of Heart **$9.95**		
A Handbook on Hope: Fusing Optimism and Action **$9.95**		
The Life of the Soul: The Path of Spirit in Your Lifetimes **$9.95**		
Available Wisdom: Insights from Beyond the Third Dimension **$9.95**		
Complete set of six books in the LifeLines Library **$39.95**		
Subtotal		
CA residents add 7.35% sales tax		
Postage and handling (F.O.B.)		
Total		

Payment Information

Charge to: VISA ☐   MasterCard ☐

Card number _____ Exp. date_____

Ship to:

Name_____

Street_____ Apt._____

City_____ State_____ Zip_____

Phone: _____ Fax_____

E-mail: _____

To order by phone call (707) 433-9771

Fax your order to (707) 433-9772

Order via e-mail at **www.fieldflowers.com**

Visit our Website at **www.lifelineslibrary.com**

LIFELINES NOTE PADS ORDER FORM

FEATURING MESSAGES FROM BOOKS IN THE LIFELINES LIBRARY

Note Pads 12 messages in each pad, 108 pages	Quantity	Total Cost @ $7.95/pad
Authenticity (#LL1000)		
Boundaries (#LL1001)		
Change (#LL1002)		
Commitment (#LL1003)		
Companionship (#LL1004)		
Courage (#LL1005)		
Effectiveness (#LL1006)		
Hope (#LL1007)		
Love (#LL1008)		
Real Work (#LL1009)		
Strength (#LL1010)		
Time (#LL1011)		
Unconditional Love (#LL1012)		
Vitality (#LL1013)		
Wisdom (#LL1014)		
Subtotal		
CA residents add 7.35% sales tax		
Postage and handling (F.O.B.)		
Total		

Payment Information

Charge to: VISA ☐   MasterCard ☐

Card number _____ Exp. date_____

Ship to:

Name_____

Street_____ Apt._____

City_____ State_____ Zip_____

Phone: _____ Fax_____

E-mail: _____

To order by phone call (707) 433-9771

Fax your order to (707) 433-9772

Order via e-mail at www.fieldflowers.com

Visit our Website at www.lifelineslibrary.com